June 2007

Dear Whitney,

May the Lord give you
Strength and endurance
to "run the race" faithfully
to the end for His glory!
2 Tim. 4:7

In His grace,
Allen + Janice

Running the Race

Running the Race

A Graduate's Guide to Life

R. C. Sproul

Baker Books

A Division of Baker Book House Co
Grand Rapids, Michigan 49516

Published by Baker Books
a division of Baker Book House Company
P.O. Box 6287, Grand Rapids, MI 49516-6287
www.bakerbooks.com

Second Printing, September 2003

Printed in the United States of America

The selections in this book are taken from the
following books by R. C. Sproul:

Lifeviews
Choosing My Religion
Choosing My Religion Student Guide
Ultimate Issues
Now, That's a Good Question!
Before the Face of God, Book Four
Before the Face of God, Book Two
Pleasing God

Permission has been granted for the use of
the following books:

Now, That's a Good Question! by R. C. Sproul
(Wheaton, Ill.: Tyndale, 1996).
Before the Face of God, Book Two by R. C.
Sproul (Grand Rapids: Baker, 1993).

Library of Congress Cataloging-in-Publication Data

Sproul, R. C. (Robert Charles), 1939–
    Running the race : a graduate's guide to what's important in life / R. C. Sproul.
        p.   cm.
    Contents: Hey! This is real life—The pragmatist: "If it works, don't fix it"—The rela-
tivist: "It's all relative"—The secularist: "You only go around once"—The hedonist: "If it
feels good, it is good"—The antinomian: "Question authority"—It's your choice—Truth?—
Fact or opinion—Truth matters—A question about reality—Living in denial—God said
it; that settles it—Ignorance is no excuse—Hogwash or the truth—God is real!—Reality
check—Dealing with the truth—It's your life—Living out what you believe—Living a
lie—Making a change—The difference God makes—God's will for you—Our job: To be
his witnesses—Running the race of life—Setting your sights on Jesus—Don't give up.
    ISBN 0-8010-1256-2
    1. Apologetics. [1. Christian life. 2. Apologetics.] I. Title.
BT1103 .S66 2003
239—dc21
                                                                      2002014335

Contents

— ONE —

Hey!
This Is
Real
Life

You've done it! You've graduated. Your whole life lies before you.

But what are you going to do now?

- Party at Daytona Beach?
- Send your application to FSU?
- Hang out with your friends?

How you answer this question largely depends on what you think is most important in life. It depends on what you value—in other words, your philosophy or worldview.

Everybody—from the college prep to the campus partier—has a worldview, a way he or she looks at the world.

In this chapter, R. C. Sproul will take you on a roller-coaster ride through the worldviews that determine how many Americans live their lives—from secularism to pragmatism, from hedonism to relativism. These worldviews, or ways of thinking, shape what we do and say. You might even be surprised by how much these worldviews influence how you live *your* life. As R. C. says, everyone must "believe in something." What do you believe?

So you're getting ready to move on. . . . Why not let R. C. introduce you to some of the people you're going to meet along the way?

The Pragmatist—"If It Works, Don't Fix It"

A student once asked me, "R. C., do you believe in God?"

"Yes," I replied.

"Are you glad that you believe that?"

"Yes."

"Does it make a difference in your life?"

"Yes, it makes a difference in my life. It helps me through all kinds of things."

The student said, "Well, I don't feel the need for God. For *you,* God is true. For *me,* there is no God. I don't need God."

What is happening here? Truth is being redefined. Truth, classically, corresponds to objectivity, to what is real. However, in pragmatism, truth is now determined by what works for me or for you. The problem arises when it works for me but it doesn't work for you. Which is true? Well, they are both true, says the pragmatist.

My discussion with the student was not about what works. My discussion was about the existence of God. I was concerned to show that if there is no God then all my praying, singing, and believing could not conjure one up. I do not have the power to create God. I can create religion, and my religious experience may be quite meaningful to me. It may "work" in the sense that it provides a bromide to help me cope with life. But it can never work to create a God if, in fact, there is no God.

On the other hand, if there is a God then the student's unbelief or disinterest in him does not have the power to destroy him. If the student finds no personal meaning in God, God's life is not thereby in jeopardy. The student is still accountable to God and will eventually face God. What turns the student on has no possible relevance to the actual existence or nonexistence of God.

Lifeviews, 83–84

Does it really matter whether Christ is real?

When someone says that Christ can be both real and imaginary, both true and false, depending on my feelings, I want to respond, "Wake up. Put your brains back in your head." He can't possibly be both. We who live in twenty-first-century America have embraced relativism and go to ridiculous lengths to apply it to religion. It is hard to believe that millions of intelligent human beings are running around saying all religions are equally true. We all know better.

Choosing My Religion, 1.22–23

I f the Bible communicates ultimate
words from almighty God, it is anything
but an occasion for recreation.

The Relativist—"It's All Relative"

To most modern people, the idea that some things are true in all places at all times for all people is, well, untrue. People are taught in the home, through the media, and in the classroom that nothing is true for everyone. Truth, it is said, is strictly relative.

Not surprisingly, this way of looking at truth is called "relativism." According to this philosophy, what's true for you is not necessarily true for anyone else. Nothing—absolutely nothing—is true for everyone.

Picture this scenario: A student at your school comes to class wearing a T-shirt that says ALL STATEMENTS ARE FALSE. That statement has a serious problem. If all statements are truly false, then his T-shirt motto must be false as well. If he really thinks his statement is true, then not *all* statements are false.

Do you see the logical knot? If the statement is true, it makes itself false. ALL STATEMENTS ARE FALSE can't possibly be true. It contradicts itself. It is, in a word, absurd.

"There is no absolute truth" is the same kind of mind bender. It's an absolute truth claim. It allows for no exceptions. It's like saying, "It's absolutely true that there is no absolute truth."

But if it's true that there is *no* absolute truth, then there's at least *one* absolute truth: "There is no absolute truth." But how can there be even one absolute truth if there are absolutely no absolute truths? Again, the statement can't possibly be true. It's self-contradictory. To affirm it is to deny it. It's absurd.

Would you base your life on the belief that all statements are false? Of course not. In fact, you would doubt the sanity of anyone who seriously asked you to believe such a joke.

Should you, then, base your life on the belief that there can be no absolute truth? Of course not. A philosophy that denies the possibility of truth is a philosophy that denies its own truth claims. And a philosophy that denies itself shouldn't be taken seriously by any thinking person.

Choosing My Religion, Student Guide, 6–7

Isn't the Bible true for some people but not for others?

Logically, this cannot be an accurate assessment of the Bible. Take, for example, the central assertion of the New Testament that Jesus Christ died and was raised from the dead. If that is true in time-and-space history for anybody, it is true for everybody. We are not talking about parallel universes, each with individual realities. One set of historical facts is true. Read any part of the New Testament and much of the Old Testament. Everything said there is predicated on the fact that a Savior would later or had in the past died and conquered death. These statements are only worthwhile if God says them, if they are so.

If they are not so—if God did not make a plan of salvation for the human race, if Jesus did not die and rise from the dead—this really is mythological fiction. Its only value is to be a historical curiosity or, as one person said it, "recreational reading." If the Bible communicates ultimate words from almighty God, it is anything but an occasion for recreation.

Ultimate Issues, 3.10

The Secularist—"You Only Go Around Once"

The secularist declares, "Right now counts for . . . right now!" There is no eternity, there is no eternal perspective. There are no absolutes. There are no abiding principles by which human life is to be judged, embraced, or evaluated. All reality is restricted or limited to the now. . . . There is no eternal purpose. The meaning of our lives is summed up by the ciphers on our tombstone: "Born 1925, died 1985." We live between two points on a calendar. We have a beginning and an ending, with no ultimate significance.

We need not go to a library and take down a dusty tome of philosophy to be exposed to the worldview of secularism. The media screams it. We think, for example, of the beer commercial that says, "You only go around once in life, so grab for all the gusto you can get." We see a man on a sailboat, the wind blowing his hair and the salt spray splashing in his face. He's having a fantastic time *right now*. Pepsi calls ours "The Now Generation." "Do it now!" "Get it now!" The message that comes through is, "You'd better get it now because there is no tomorrow ultimately." Life is to be consumed in the present. Our philosophy must be a philosophy of the immediate.

The secularists of Jesus' day summed up their philosophy like this: "Eat, drink, and be merry. For tomorrow you die." Contrast that with Jesus' words: "Lay up for yourselves treasures in heaven." Think in terms of eternity. Think of the long-range implications. This touches us most directly, not simply in how we handle our bank accounts, but at the level of how we invest our lives. Life is an investment, and the question that modern man has to answer is, "Am I going to invest my life for short-term benefits or for long-term gains?"

Lifeviews, 36–37

Why does God let random shootings, fatal accidents, and other horrible things occur?

Death and suffering entered the world as a direct result of sin. . . .

The Bible makes it clear that God lets these things happen and in a certain sense ordains that they come to pass as part of the present situation that is under judgment. He has not removed death from this world. Whether it's what we would consider an untimely death or a violent death, death is part of the nature of things. The only promise is that there will come a day when suffering will cease altogether.

The disciples asked Jesus about similar instances—for example, the Galileans' blood that was mingled with the sacrifices by Pilate or the eighteen people who were killed when a temple collapsed. The disciples asked how this could be. Jesus' response was almost severe. He said, "Unless you repent, you will all likewise perish," again bringing the question back to the fact that moral wickedness makes it feasible for God to allow these kinds of dreadful things to take place in a fallen world (Luke 13:1–5 NKJV).

Now, That's a Good Question! 30–31

We were created for God.
Just as fish are in despair out of water,
so the human soul is in despair
when it is outside of fellowship
with God.

The Hedonist—"If It Feels Good, It Is Good"

Hedonism makes a value judgment by saying that the avoidance of pain and the pursuit of pleasure are good. At the same time, it produces a system of ethics which, in turn, produces a certain behavioral pattern of morality. A popular maxim of our culture is "If it feels good, it is good." Goodness is determined by feeling. Popular music communicates the message that the final test of what is right is the feeling test.

The sexual revolution is rooted in [this] hedonistic ethic. A recent quote from author Helen Gurley Brown indicates how much our society has been influenced by hedonism. She has given us a new definition of promiscuity. In the fifties the word *promiscuity* meant "having sexual relationships with more than one person, outside of marriage." The new definition by Helen Gurley Brown is "having sexual relationships with more than one person *in the same day.*" Catch that phrase "*in the same day.*" That is the new definition of promiscuity. We must understand that the sexual revolution our nation has experienced has not happened in a vacuum. There are cultural and philosophical reasons for these changes.

At the root, hedonism is a philosophy of despair. It reflects a deep-seated sense of hopelessness of people trapped on this side of the wall. It is a quasi-logical conclusion to secularism. If my life is bound by the poles of birth and death, if my life has no eternal significance, then why not grab whatever pleasure I can squeeze out of my brief time on earth? If death is ultimate and life is meaningless, we need an escape. Temporary euphoria seems better than none at all. The cocaine high, the sexual orgasm, the gourmet meal all offer at least a brief respite from constant despair. The final creed of the hedonist is "Eat, drink, and be merry, for tomorrow we die."

The ancient Epicurean and the modern hedonist both search for the same thing—peace of mind. They are looking for relief that goes beyond Rolaids. Peace of mind, however, is elusive. The deepest desire of man is for a stable peace, a peace that lasts without giving way to a hangover.

Saint Augustine was a crass hedonist before his conversion to Christianity. He pursued the sensuous route; he was a pleasure seeker. His famous prayer, penned after his conversion, expressed the human dilemma: "O God, thou has created us for Thyself, and our hearts are restless until they find their rest in Thee."

Augustine saw a link between human restlessness, a gnawing form of anxiety, and living against the purpose of our creation. We were created for God. Just as fish are in despair out of water, so the human soul is in despair when it is outside of fellowship with God. The Westminster Catechism asks: "What is man's chief end?" The answer provided is: "Man's chief end is to glorify God and to enjoy Him forever."

The goal of man is God. He is the fountain of peace, the wellspring of joy. We were created for happiness, not gloom. We were created for hope, not despair.

Lifeviews, 136–37

Why won't God accept me as I am? He's loving and good, isn't he?

Again, we have turned off our minds. We have forgotten what it means to be good. Paul told the Romans that God's judgment is based on truth—ultimate truth. Paul means that if God really is good, he has no option but wrath. A just, holy judge who winks at evil and refuses to punish it is not a just, holy judge. That sort of judge wouldn't be worth respecting. He wouldn't be consistent to the law or what he believed to be right.

Choosing My Religion, 3.14

The Antinomian—"Question Authority"

Franky MacKendrick screeches to a halt in front of the tennis courts in his brand-new BMW 325. He downs the last hit of his brewsky while rocking to the Guns 'n' Roses CD thundering out of his Blaupunkt stereo at a volume deadly to infants and small animals. QUESTION AUTHORITY reads the prominently displayed bumper sticker.

Franky is a twenty-four-year-old financial wizard. He's got an Ivy League degree and a prestigious job. But though Franky has accomplished much for his years, he's got a major problem: He's an *antinomian*—he's against the law. (In Greek, *anti* means "against" and *nomos* means "law.")

Franky isn't merely against any particular laws—such as laws regulating the speed limit, drinking while driving, or the volume of car stereos. No, Franky is against the whole idea of law. As far as Franky is concerned, he's his own authority, and nobody can tell him what to do. Period.

Franky isn't alone. You live in a world that is radically antinomian. From your earliest days, your culture has been trying to convince you that you have to determine your own laws for yourself, apart from any external authority.

But to look at the world truthfully—to have a biblical worldview—you have to reject that idea. You have to see God as having ultimate authority. And you have to see God's authority as revealed to you through God's Word and the world.

And that's why true Christians—those whose possession of faith matches their profession of faith—will respect God's authority. And because they respect God's authority, they will obey the laws of the Bible and the laws of men (Rom. 13:1–6)—as long as the laws of men don't contradict the laws in the Bible, of course (Acts 4:19–20; 5:29).

I guess that means someone needs to manufacture a new bumper sticker, one that reads SUBMIT TO AUTHORITY. . . . Nah. It would never sell.

Choosing My Religion Student Guide, 35–36

Why do Christians seem so judgmental?

I've often said that every nonbeliever in America knows one verse that's in the Bible: "Judge not, that ye be not judged" (Matt. 7:1 KJV), and they appeal to that by saying that nobody ever has the right to say that anything they do is wrong. For a judge in a courtroom to declare an accused person guilty of a crime is not judgmental. For a Christian to recognize sinful behavior in another Christian or non-Christian as sinful is not judgmental.

To be judgmental in the sense in which it's prohibited in Scripture is to manifest a censorious attitude, a pharisaic attitude of condemning people out of hand and consigning them to utter worthlessness because of their sin, without any spirit of patience, forbearance, kindness, or mercy.

That's why Jesus warns us about noticing the speck in our brother's eye when we have a log in our own eye. The person who is running around examining specks is a person who has this judgmental spirit that Jesus found absolutely abhorrent. That doesn't mean that we are to be loose on sin or to call good evil or evil good. *Judgmental* describes an attitude.

Now, That's a Good Question! 516

Paul told the Romans that God's judgment is based on truth—ultimate truth.

It's Your Choice

Every man and woman at some time in life comes to the point of turning toward one truth to the exclusion of all competing truths. Before us lie all options of beliefs on which we may base our lives. The fact that we all make this choice (and choosing not to choose is a choice) is one indication that there is a correct path somewhere. There is one existential reality, and you and I are part of that reality. It exists and holds things together. No reality we can comprehend exists in a totally contradictory universe, with no absolute truths. Even Isaac Asimov could not turn such a universe into a science fiction novel. Its reality would change from page to page. Fortunately, even the relativist makes assumptions based on a shared, consistent reality in which certain truths are true.

That doesn't mean the system you choose must be consistent, logical, or even rational. It can tie your mind up in knots. But you must choose, and that choice will be your religion. You will come to complete the sentence: "I believe in . . ." You may come to rechoose later, and affirm: "I used to believe in . . . , but now I believe in . . ." At each point you will believe in something, and that belief will shape your loves, hates, ideals, behavior, and goals. Your life's pattern, and most of its choices, will be determined in that moment you complete the sentence: "I believe in . . ."

Choosing My Religion, 1.6–7

— TWO —

Truth?

Does truth really matter?

Truth certainly matters if you're going to find out who scraped the finish on your brand-new Jetta. But does truth really matter when it comes to living out your life?

In this chapter, R. C. makes the case for truth.

Fact or Opinion

Does truth matter, or is everything relative? Let me begin to suggest an answer to those questions by inviting you to participate in a quiz. There are two questions. To make things interesting, let's imagine that if you answer either question correctly you will win a Mitsubishi Eclipse (4-cylinder, 140 hp, with CD deck and a sun roof? Hey, why not?).

The first question is simple: A large glass jar filled with jelly beans sits on the table before you. *How many pieces of candy are in the jar?*

I wonder if that physics lesson on mass and displacement would be of help here. Probably not. Finally all contestants have written down their answers. Ready for question 2:

What is the best flavor of ice cream?

Where is Baskin-Robbins when you need them? You mean which flavor is the most popular? Which flavor sells best?

Simply name the *best* flavor.

All answers written down?

How many jelly beans are in the jar? One guess comes in at 250, another at 500, and another at 643. One joker has guessed there are 55,732—and one-half. Your guess was 412. The actual number of beans: 413.

All right! . . . Just toss over those ignition keys!

No can do. No one guessed correctly. There was an actual number of beans in the jar, and you did not come up with that number. Close doesn't count.

Maybe someone did better on the second question. Answers are varied: Strawberry Swirl. Mackinac Island Fudge. The ever-popular Vanilla. Neapolitan.

Isn't Neapolitan three flavors?

Oh, that's from the guy with the 55,000-plus jelly beans.

The correct answer is: There is no correct answer. The *best* flavor of ice cream is the flavor you personally prefer. It is really just a matter of personal preference or the flavor you associate in your mind with pleasant memories, the one you shared with that cute sophomore and now gives you warm fuzzies when you think of it.

Choosing My Religion, 1.4–5

[That's the difference between facts and opinions. Facts deal with reality. The jar actually contains a certain, specific number of jelly beans—no more, no less. For questions concerning ultimate reality, there's a right answer and a wrong answer. And in the end, what kind of answer you give does matter.]

Truth Matters

If an objective reality stands behind life, that reality defines the way the world functions. Attempts to bypass this reality should carry the surgeon general's warning: "Ignoring truth is hazardous to your life and sanity." I do not want to drive across a bridge designed by an engineer who believed the numbers in structural stress models are relative truths. Things follow rules, or an authority structure. Chemical elements do not change the way they interact without good reason. Program a computer with the equations to account for variables it will encounter, and the computer will tick off astoundingly complex formulations with minute accuracy. It works because we can trust in the absolute authority of the laws governing reality.

Absolute truth, then, empowers us. Once we learn what the truth is as well as its structure of authority, we can move out confidently, trusting in the authority structure that governs life. Functioning in a world without absolute truth and the authority behind it would be a hideous experience. We could trust nothing.

Choosing My Religion, 1.12

Isn't it being narrow-minded for Christians to say Christ is the only way?

I'll never forget the first time somebody asked me that. I was in college, and my college professor looked me straight in the eye and said, "Mr. Sproul, do you believe that Jesus is the only way to God?" I wanted to jump out the window or find a hole to hide in. . . . I knew that Jesus himself had said, "I am the way and the truth and the life. No one comes to the Father except through me" (John 14:6).

This professor pressed me on it and asked if I thought Jesus was the only way. If I said yes, then obviously I would be understood by everybody in the class to be an unspeakably arrogant person. I certainly didn't want that kind of a label during my college career. But if I said no, then I would be guilty of denying that unique exclusiveness that Christ claimed for himself. So I kind of hedged a little bit and tried to whisper my answer and said, "Yes, I believe that Jesus is the only way." Well, the wrath of that teacher came on my head, and the teacher just began to lay me out and said, "That's the most bigoted, narrow-minded, arrogant statement I have ever heard."

When the class was over, I went up to the professor and spoke privately to her. "I know you're not enthusiastic about Christianity, but do you allow for the possibility that people who are not arrogant and people who are not narrow minded could for some reason or other actually be persuaded that Jesus Christ is at least one way to God?" The professor said, "Oh yes, I can certainly understand that intelligent people could believe that." . . . I said, "Don't you understand that I came to the conclusion that Jesus was *a* way to God, and then I discovered that Jesus was saying that he is *the* way?"

Now, That's a Good Question! 140–41

Refusal to acknowledge what you know to be true is the primary sin of the heart.

A Question about Reality

On a college campus I was debating with a young woman the question: "Does God exist?" She finally turned to me and asked, "Well, Professor Sproul, do you find religion meaningful?"

"Yes."

"Do you pray to God?"

"Yes."

"Do you like to sing hymns?"

"Yes."

"Do you go to church on Sunday morning?"

"Yes."

"Do you engage in fellowship activities?"

"Yes."

"Well then, since this is all so wonderful and meaningful for you, then for you God exists. But that's irrelevant to me and to my life. I don't find any meaning whatsoever in praying or going to church or singing hymns or doing any of that religious stuff. So for me, there is no God."

I was honestly confused by her reasoning.

"I'm not talking about my religious experience or your religious experience. We're discussing the question of whether in reality there is such a being whom we call God. If God does not exist in reality, all my praying, all my singing, all my preaching, all my church-going activities, all of that stuff won't have the power to conjure him up. I can't create him. If he does exist apart from me and apart from you, all of your unbelief, all of your disinterest, does not have the power to kill him."

Choosing My Religion, 1.19–20

Living in Denial

[The apostle] Paul writes that every human who contemplates the created world knows what kind of God is there. The tragedy is that people prefer to live in denial. They refuse to admit to a knowledge of God because they do not want to admit their dependence on God. "For although they knew God, they neither glorified him as God nor gave thanks to him, but their thinking became futile and their foolish hearts were darkened. . . . They exchanged the truth of God for a lie, and worshiped and served created things rather than the Creator—who is forever praised" (Rom. 1:21, 25).

This is a stunning indictment. Paul is not talking about atheism. He describes a human religion that robs the God who is. Here is the scene Paul describes: I walk into an exhibition of European masterpieces, look around a bit, select a Peter Paul Rubens portrait, and remove it from the wall. Immediately, alarm sirens scream and thirty-two guards level guns at my head. But I refuse to let any of that bother me.

"What do you think you are doing?" the curator asks.

"This slab was hanging there. It's kind of colorful, and I thought it might make a nice welcome mat outside my back door."

"But this is worth millions of dollars. You may come to this museum to enjoy it. But what makes you think you can just take it away?"

"I do not believe that this is any more than a piece of flotsam that happens to have a pleasing shape and colors. It almost looks like somebody could have made it, but I refuse to accept any such fiction. I even refuse to accept that all that horrendous noise made a few moments ago has any connection with the fact that I pulled this thing off that wall, where it had no particular reason to be anyway."

Rubens has been dead many years and is not personally injured if I refuse to acknowledge his creation of a painting. . . . I would far rather rob Rubens of the glory due him than rob a living God of his rightful majesty, of his transcendent power, of his deity. Paul is saying that we know quite well that a Creator Deity exists, yet the universal human reaction is refusal to honor God or to be grateful. Refusal to acknowledge what you know to be true is the primary sin of the heart.

You know that you are not God.

You know that you are a creature.

You know that you are finite, derived, and dependent.

You know that you are morally responsible for your behavior. At a specific moment in history you will stand before your Creator to give an account of your behavior.

If all that is true, then why do we refuse to honor God? Certainly, the problem is not that God is intrinsically dishonorable. We owe everything we have to his being. Every good gift we enjoy comes from his benevolence. But we refuse to honor God as God.

Ultimate Issues, 2.13–15

Didn't the universe just evolve into being? How can I really believe God created it?

I am personally intrigued by "Big Bang" cosmology. I find it fascinating and not necessarily incompatible with the Bible's account of creation. But there are those who take speculation about origins a step further to say that the universe came into being by itself, accidentally, or perhaps it was already there from all eternity. Either explanation takes a lot more faith than to postulate that God created it all. In Romans 1 Paul regards it as intellectual dishonesty. The common purpose of wicked people is to come up with some explanation, any explanation, to avoid the assertion of a Creator.

Ultimate Issues, 2.10

God Said It; That Settles It

You have probably seen cars with religion-promoting bumper stickers. Some Christians like to decorate their cars with bumper-sticker messages. One popular message says, "God said it. I believe it. That settles it." This bumper sticker is bad theology. Its middle clause ignores the difference between a Creator God and those who have been created. If the Creator God says it, it is settled—whether I believe it or not. If the supremely powerful Source of ultimate truth opens his sacred mouth and utters a single word, debate is moot. The question is not whether the matter is settled once God says it.

The question is whether he has said anything. In Christianity the issue revolves around the Bible. We set the Bible apart in our thinking as *the Scriptures.* The word means "writings," but in terms of Christian faith the Scriptures are the only writings that come from the mouth of God. We commit absolutely everything to the proposition that a Creator exists, wants to be heard, and has spoken.

Ultimate Issues, 3.7

Why should I trust the Bible?

Does the Bible communicate reliable, historical information?

On the basis of any accepted measure of historical verification (for example, contemporary corroboration from multiple and disinterested sources, archeological and textual evidence, and evidence of identifiable impact on people or institutions), no individual in history is better attested to than Jesus of Nazareth. To dismiss all that demonstrates unworthy research bias.

Scripture's testimony is at least as reliable as the work of the ancient historians Tacitus or Heroditus. Abraham Herschel, a modern Judaic theologian and archeologist, singled out the writer of the Gospel of Luke and the Acts for special note. Luke, said Herschel, is the most trustworthy historian of antiquity. For such a knowledgeable non-Christian to make that statement is significant.

Ultimate Issues, 3.12

The Bible is the only certain map by which to chart travel toward answers to ultimate questions.

Ignorance Is No Excuse

If we don't struggle with the Word of God it is only because we are so ignorant of it. Ignorance of Scripture is pervasive in our culture. Why? The primary reason is that the subject is ignored. We ignore the Bible. We don't want to think about God. We want to banish him from intruding, particularly when he makes a claim on our lives and impulses. In my natural self it is easier if there are no ultimate realities in a revealed word from God. I prefer that such a revelation be a myth because I want to be free of its obligation. I have a conflict over the ultimate issue of authority. If I exercise personal autonomy, I am a law unto myself. I can do anything I want because I want.

If that is where we are, we had better hope that there is no God and no law or that God is dumb and deaf and blind.

But don't bet your life on it.

Ultimate Issues, 3.18

What does Jesus say about the Bible?

Critics have never found legitimate reason to challenge most of Jesus' own comments about the integrity of Scripture. Passages in which Jesus declares that the Scriptures are the Word of God are seldom tagged as inauthentic. Even most skeptics believe that the historical person of Jesus of Nazareth made such statements as the following:

> Everything must be fulfilled that is written about me in the Law of Moses, the Prophets and the Psalms.
>
> Luke 24:44

> The Scripture cannot be broken.
>
> John 10:35

> You diligently study the Scriptures because you think that by them you possess eternal life. These are the Scriptures that testify about me, yet you refuse to come to me to have life.
>
> John 5:39–40

> *Ultimate Issues*, 3.14–15

Hogwash or the Truth

Conversation around the coffeehouse table should stimulate creative thinking and understanding. Unfortunately, sometimes it generates pooled idiocy. You probably have experienced the latter sort of discussion. Camaraderie may be warm. Everyone has a view to throw out onto the floor—until you are all ankle-deep in hogwash. No one has done the thinking needed to formulate a meaningful opinion, let alone sustain it by logical arguments. That is no way to approach ultimate issues.

Sure answers to the ultimate questions of life *are* available. . . . There is much to learn from the accumulated wisdom of human history. But the Bible is the only certain map by which to chart travel toward answers to *ultimate* questions. The Bible serves as a fixed reference point from which to distinguish truth among the sayings of the wise. It is the instruction manual for life. . . . I am elated by that news, until I read what the revelation contained in the Bible says.

It tells me that life is screwed up.

It tells me that God is angry at the reasons life is screwed up.

It tells me that I am one of the reasons life is screwed up.

In bold letters the Manufacturer's advisory reads,

WARNING
Small is the gate and
narrow the road that
leads to life,
and only a few
find it.

Imagine reading this sign and suddenly realizing you are standing on a tiny piece of firm ground in the center of a quicksand bog. There's one narrow path out, and it can be seen only by aligning your line of sight on a distant gate. Any deviation from this unseen path leads to disaster. Would you be motivated to hold your sights on the gate, accepting no substitutes?

Ultimate Issues, 4.4–5

God Is Real!

The kingdom of God is real. At this very moment Jesus sits in the seat of cosmic authority. He is now the supreme ruler of the world. He stands over the governments of this world. He is King. The Premier of the Soviet Union must answer to him. The Dalai Lama of Tibet must answer to him. The Prince of Morocco must answer to him. The President of the United States must answer to him. But there is one big problem. His kingdom is *invisible*. Not everyone knows about it. All over the world people are living as if Jesus were not King.

Some people believe that there is no God. Others say that there are many gods. Some folks believe that man is supreme. Others believe that man is worthless. Many people believe there is a God, but they live as if there were no God. Still others ask, "What difference does it make?"

Where Christ is invisible, people perish. Where his reign is unknown or ignored, people are exploited. They are demeaned. They are enslaved. They are butchered. They are aborted. They are raped. They are casualties of war. They are robbed. They are slandered. They are oppressed. They are cheated in marriage. They are cheated in their wages. They are left to go hungry, naked, and unsheltered. They are consigned to loneliness. They are ridiculed. They are frightened—that and a whole lot more, is what difference it makes.

In all of life's situations we are to be his witnesses. Our job is to *make the invisible reign of Jesus visible.* The world is shrouded in darkness. Nothing is visible in the dark. No wonder then that we are called to be the light of the world. Every single one of us has a mission. We have all been sent to bear witness to Christ. That means simply that we are all missionaries.

Lifeviews, 19–20

Why is God invisible?

I don't think there's anything that makes living the Christian life more difficult than the fact that the Lord we serve is invisible to us. You know the expression in our culture "Out of sight, out of mind." It's very, very difficult to live your life dedicated to someone or something you cannot see. . . .

Scriptures tell us uniformly that no person shall see God and live; this is because God is holy, and we are not (see Exod. 33:20; 1 Tim. 6:16). Even Moses, as righteous as he was, pleaded with God on the mountain to let him have an unveiled look at God's glory. God only allowed him to catch a refracted glimpse of God's back parts, but he said to Moses, "My face shall not be seen." Ever since Adam and Eve fell and were driven from the Garden, God has been invisible to human beings, but not because God is intrinsically incapable of being seen. The problem is not with our eyes but with our hearts.

Now, That's a Good Question! 9–10

*I*f you confess your sins and bow yourself
in submission, and rely on Christ's righteousness
instead of your own, then God promises you
the total cleansing of yourself in his sight,
the right to become a child of God.

Reality Check

Some say, "Religion is fine for you, but you have to understand that *I don't need Jesus.*" When I hear that, I realize I am talking with someone who has fallen asleep to reality. I can understand that a person might say to me, "R. C., I don't want Jesus." But when they say, "R. C., I don't need Jesus," I ask, "Have you lost your mind? Do you hear what you're saying?"

If there's no God, of course you don't need Jesus. If there is a God, and he is holy and you are holy, you don't need Jesus. But if God is and God is holy, and you are not holy, there is nothing in this universe you need more desperately than Jesus. A holy God will never negotiate justice. His justice must be satisfied or he is no longer good. He is no longer just. He is no longer holy. He is no longer God.

There are only two ways that God's justice can be satisfied with respect to your sin. Either you satisfy it or

Christ satisfies it. You can satisfy it by being banished from God's presence forever. Or you can accept the satisfaction that Jesus Christ has made. Jesus was God. God had to go to the cross himself to pay the price.

Choosing My Religion, 3.20

Dealing with the Truth

Most people are unaware of one of two things. Many aren't aware of either of them.

First, they don't know who God is.

Second, they don't know who they are.

God is perfect and we are not. And our righteousness is not righteousness enough. The Old Testament prophet Isaiah said all of our own righteousness is like filthy rags when we place them before the standard of authentic righteousness (Isa. 64:6). That's why the only way a human being can possibly stand before God is that he must be clothed with true righteousness. The only supply source I know for that is Jesus Christ.

When Martin Luther said that justification is by faith alone, he meant that justification is trusting in the righteousness of Christ—in the righteousness of Christ alone. This is the message of grace. This is the provision that God has made for you. He has made no other.

If you confess your sins and bow yourself in submission, and rely on Christ's righteousness instead of your own, then God promises you the total cleansing of yourself in his sight, the right to become a child of God (John 1:12–13).

That's the gospel.

What you do with it is the ultimate issue.

Ultimate Issues, 4.17–18

If I'm happy with my life, why do I need Jesus?

I hear that from a lot of folks. They say to me, "I just don't feel the need for Christ." As if Christianity were something that were packaged and sold through Madison Avenue! That what we're trying to communicate to people is "Here's something that's going to make you feel good, and everybody needs a little of this in their closet or in their refrigerator," as if it were some commodity that's going to add a dash of happiness to our lives.

If the only reason a human being ever needed Jesus was to be happy and a person is already happy without Jesus, then they certainly don't need Jesus. The New Testament indicates, however, that there's another reason you or somebody else needs Jesus. There is a God who is altogether holy, who is perfectly just, and who declares that he is going to judge the world and hold every human being accountable for their life. As a perfectly holy and just God, he requires from each one of us a life of perfect obedience and of perfect justness. . . .

The problem is simply this: If God is just and requires perfection from me, and I come short of that perfection and he is going to deal with me according to justice, then I am looking at a future punishment at the hands of a holy God. If the only way I can escape punishment is through a Savior, and if I want to escape that, then I need a Savior.

Now, That's a Good Question! 110–11

— THREE —

It's Your Life

Okay, what does all this talk about truth have to do with your life? You've got all kinds of important decisions to make—decisions about your career, your education, whom you're going to date, or whom you will marry. Does God have anything to say about those things? Should believing in Jesus make any difference in how you live your life today?

In this chapter, R. C. explores the intimate connection between your beliefs and your life. Along the way, he hands out some helpful hints on how you can discover God's will and align your life with it.

It's your life. How are you going to live it?

Living Out What You Believe

Most of us are inconsistent about such matters. Our viewpoint comes from the melting pot. We get mixed up. Our pot has a dash of faith and a dash of skepticism. We are at once religious and secular. We believe in God, sometimes. Our religion has elements of superstition at some times and is tempered by sober science at other times. We are at the same time Christians and card-carrying pragmatists. On Sunday we say the creed. On Monday we are fatalists. We try to separate our religious life from the rest of our life. We live by holding contradictory beliefs. Living in contradictions can be exciting. Life is surely more than logic. But the contradictory life is a confusing life, a life of inconsistency and incoherence. Its bottom line is chaos.

We are inconsistent and confused because we fail to understand where Christianity ends and paganism begins. We do not know where the boundary lines are.

Consequently we traffic back and forth across the lines, making forays between darkness and light. We are lost in our own culture, swirling around in the melting pot while somebody else has his hand on the spoon. We're not sure whether we are the witnesses or the ones being witnessed to. We don't know if we are the missionaries or the mission field.

It was Socrates who said that the unexamined life is not worth living. To examine one's life is to think about it. It is to *evaluate*. To evaluate requires examining values and value systems. We all have values. We all have some viewpoint about what life is all about. We all have some perspective on the world we live in. We are not all philosophers but we all have a philosophy. Perhaps we haven't thought much about that philosophy, but one thing is certain—we live it out. How we live reveals our deepest convictions about life. Our lives say much more about how we think than our books do. The theories we preach are not always the ones we actually believe. The theories we live are the ones we really believe.

Lifeviews, 25–26

Living a Lie

A pastor told me of his concern about a young man who attended meetings of the youth group. This guy habitually used drugs and was living with a girl. The pastor confronted the young man, asking him, "Don't you realize that this lifestyle is totally unacceptable to God?" The man answered, "What's the big deal? Everybody else is doing it."

The two came to an impasse. The pastor was saying that God's standard isn't what "everybody else is doing," that there are things God forbids. The young man was saying, "Hey, don't worry about it. I don't need to be obedient to God. I'm quite happy being a carnal (worldly) Christian. I'm Christian enough."

No, he's not Christian enough. He is not a Christian at all, and he too is in for a rude awakening, now or when he faces God. The prodigal son was awakened and resolved to leave the old life behind. He left the pigsty that day. He still smelled like pigs and he still had pig manure all over his clothes. You don't get rid of the stain of the pigs in five minutes. That's the struggle of the Christian life. Every now and then we still long for Daytona Beach freedom; we may take a quick tour through the pigpen. We can still mess up big time because we haven't gotten over our fascination with the pigs. But we can't take up residence with [pigs] and pretend to be Christians.

Choosing My Religion, 4.15

If you truly embrace the holiness of God and love and delight in the majesty of God you will be unwilling and unable not to change.

Making a Change

There's a pernicious idea going through this land that a person can become a Christian without making [a] radical change. The reasoning goes something like this: I can accept Jesus as my Savior now, and I can accept him as Lord in control of my thoughts and actions later. Because Jesus died to release me from living under law, I have God's grace. He forgives all my sins no matter what. So it doesn't really matter how I live. I can accept Jesus as the Lord of my life, or not. It is a separate decision that has nothing to do with my salvation.

Perhaps you know someone who believes that. Perhaps you have believed it. Or perhaps you or someone you know has rejected Christianity because Christians behave no differently from anyone else. Whatever the case, there is not one person who truly has Jesus as Christ but does not turn over all of life to him now and forever. . . .

Therefore, don't believe it. You cannot stay in the pigsty if you are a Christian. If you truly embrace the holiness of God, and love and delight in the majesty of God you will be unwilling and unable not to change. You won't have it all together immediately, or ever. None of us lives without sin. But neither can anyone stay in the far country of open rebellion against God.

Choosing My Religion, 4.12–13

The Difference God Makes

Let's imagine for a moment that after establishing the conviction that a Creator-Ruler God really exists, you are awakened by the red-orange glow of a sunrise shining through the window. Contemplating the view from bed, you are struck by the beauty of the design of a sunrise.

The alternative: "Lot of dust floating around out there today."

Should you get up? The tasks awaiting you at work don't promise much excitement. But that's all right. Even dull days are gifts that can be enjoyed.

The alternatives: (1) Another day, another dollar to keep the wolf from the door. (2) Wonder how many sick days I have left? I think I'll take one and just sleep in.

The morning paper tells about a comet colliding with Jupiter. Oh, well, thank heaven things are under control!

The alternative: There's always something new to worry about. What's the point of things when we may go up like a cosmic firecracker next week? . . .

Those sorts of thoughts and decisions are rattling through your head and it isn't even eight o'clock in the morning. Not every choice is conscious or involves ethical issues. . . . The atheist can enjoy the colorful sunrise, but not as a created, designed thing. The theist may worry over what is in the news, but a consistent theist works from the assumption that what is reported is not a random act of blind chance.

The theist thinks *theocentrically;* the reality of God moves toward the center of all that is evaluated and analyzed. *God* is an idea with enormous implications.

Ultimate Issues, 1.10–11

How can I find wisdom?

We [certainly] need wisdom in the midst of trials and circumstances [of this life]. James [reminds] us that God gives wisdom freely (James 1:5). He has told us where we can find wisdom—in the Scriptures. God gives the perfect gifts of life and wisdom through his Word. We need the power of life in order to combat the inner uprisings of temptation. We need the wisdom of God to see his larger purposes in the difficulties and trials he graciously sends our way to shape and mature us.

Therefore, we should be quick to listen and slow to speak. There is a place to speak. . . . [But] on balance, we should listen a lot more than we speak.

Before the Face of God, Book Four, 398

Who you are in Christ is far more significant than the details of vocation, marriage, and geography.

God's Will for You

People often ask me to help them discern God's will for their lives. I have to answer, "If you are asking me how you can know whether God wants you to live in Chattanooga or St. Louis, or whether to marry Sally or Becky, that's a difficult question. But I can tell you this: The will of God for your life is your sanctification. Make the kingdom of God and his righteousness the main goal, for God is far more concerned about that than whether you live in a particular city or whether you marry a particular person."

Who you are in Christ is far more significant than the details of vocation, marriage, and geography. Those concerns are far more satisfactorily determined when a person is growing in faith, holiness, and obedience.

God requires us to walk by faith, which means to walk trusting him. First, he calls on us to act justly, to do what is right. If we trust him, we will obey him. We will be a people who avoid sin and pursue righteousness. Sometimes doing things justly is painful and risky, but if we trust God we will do what is right anyway.

Second, he calls on us to love mercy. The word here translated "mercy" can be translated "lovingkindness," "steadfast love," or "to love with loyalty." Are we loyal in our love for those around us, or are we fickle?

We could it put it this way: Are we trustworthy? If God is trustworthy we are supposed to be trustworthy also. How many of us have been deeply hurt because we confided something in a friend, only to have that friend betray our trust? More important, have we betrayed confidences and shown ourselves to be untrustworthy? We want others to be merciful to us and to guard our confidences. Just so, we must be merciful to others.

Third, he calls on us to walk humbly with our God. We can afford to walk with God because he is completely trustworthy. We can open up to him in prayer because he will never betray us. We can submit to him because he will never cause us to come to any real harm, even when he chastises us.

Before the Face of God, Book Two, 184–85

Should all Christians consider full-time Christian work?

In the modern church we make a distinction between the "professional missionary" and the "layman." The distinction is between paid missionaries and volunteers, between "full-time" hired employees and rank-and-file church members. Sadly, it has come to mean that the paid professionals are responsible to do the missions task. The layperson's job is to pray for the missionary, give tithes to the missionary, and in other ways encourage the missionary. The missionaries are the players; the rest of us are cheerleaders.

God teaches us otherwise. Of course there is a special place for the paid professional. However, the biblical definition of a missionary has nothing to do with salary. A missionary is not simply "one who is paid." In biblical terms a missionary is "one who is *sent.*" Here is the crux of the matter. We are all sent. It is our calling to be witnesses. Every Christian must get in the game. There are no cheerleaders—only players.

Lifeviews, 17–18

Our Job: To Be His Witnesses

Suppose for a moment that you had the opportunity to meet Jesus face to face. If in that meeting you had the chance to ask Jesus one question, what would you ask him? The disciples had the opportunity to ask Jesus questions every day. They asked him how to pray, how to heal the sick, and questions about theology. There came a moment, however, when they were down to their last question. They stood with Jesus on the Mount of Olives, the mountain of ascension. Jesus was about to depart from them. The cloud of Shekinah glory was ready to envelop Christ and lift him to heaven. Jesus was leaving this planet.

There was time for one more question. What was it? The disciples asked, "Lord, are you at this time going to restore the kingdom to Israel?" (Acts 1:6). I wonder why they asked that question. Wouldn't it be nice if Jesus had answered, "Yes. The work is finished. I am going to the right hand of the Father. As soon as I arrive and am enthroned as King of kings and Lord of lords you can all enjoy a vacation. I'll take care of everything. I'll make sure that every element of the world recognizes my reign. We will make an official announcement by writing it in the sky. Then I will send angels to every remote part of the globe to make absolutely certain that everybody knows that I am now the king of the universe. You fellows take a rest. Go back up in the stands and enjoy the game."

We know that is not what Jesus said. Rather he answered their question something like this: "Look, it's none of your business *when* the kingdom is going to be restored to Israel. My Father has a timetable for that. What *is* your business is to *be my witnesses.*"

Lifeviews, 18–19

What should I do when I'm trying to make an important decision—such as a career decision?

I think the most significant thing we're called to do when we're seeking the will of God in our lives, whether it's for our vocation or for our choice of a mate or where we're to live, is to think. Now, *how* are we to think? In what *way* are we to think? The Bible tells us that we ought to make a sober analysis of our gifts and talents. We recognize in doing so that it is God who gives us the gifts. It is God who gives us the talent, and it is God whom we are trying to serve and whom we want to please. That's why we want to discern what his will is for our vocation. How do we make a sober analysis of our gifts and talents? We have to think, and we have to think deeply and accurately. We can get some help in this process. We are encouraged by Scripture to seek the counsel of others because usually our gifts are recognized by the body of Christ. People in our church, in our family, and in our circle of friends have a tendency to call attention to the gifts we display. . . .

Sometimes we get forced into patterns of jobs or careers where we have the skills, we have the talents, but we really don't have the desire or the motivation to apply ourselves 100 percent. I grant that it's possible God could call us to a task we hate to perform, but God is a much better manager than that. For his jobs in this world, I think God likes to hire the people who not only have the gifts he gave them and the talent he gave them but who are motivated in those directions. Somehow, I think one of the great lies of Satan is to tell us that we are supposed to be unhappy with our labor. God has called you to be fulfilled in your labor, so it's perfectly legitimate to ask yourself, What can I do that fulfills me?

Now, That's a Good Question! 413–14

$\mathcal{J}$esus went through cross and trial; so will you. He was crowned with glory and honor; by his grace you will be.

Running the Race of Life

Runners in relay events customarily carry a baton around the track, passing it from teammate to teammate to the finish line. The baton makes the difference between success and failure. The fastest runners may lose if they fumble (or worse, drop) the baton. After Elijah had run his difficult race, God commanded that he pass his prophetic mission to Elisha (2 Kings 2:1–15). But it wasn't enough for Elisha to move into the prophetic office. They had to exchange the baton of faith.

Elijah's faith had a physical symbol. His work for God evidently had been so identified with the cloak he wore, that God chose the mantle as proof of Elisha's commission.

When it came time for Elijah to be taken into heaven, he and Elisha were at Gilgal. Elijah suggested that Elisha remain, but Elisha insisted on going along to Bethel. At

Bethel and Jericho Elisha again refused to stop. He crossed the Jordan with Elijah into the wilderness.

Elisha was preparing for the handoff. He knew that it was important for the rest of the prophets to see them together. He also loved Elijah and wanted to extend his learning from the master until the last moment. When Elijah asked if Elisha had a last request to make of him, Elisha knew an intimidating responsibility would momentarily be his. If he were to follow in Elijah's footsteps, he would need the strength of the Spirit of God. So he boldly asked for a double portion—the eldest son's share—of Elijah's spirit.

Elijah replied that this would be difficult. God could easily give strength, but could Elisha bear to receive it? A double measure of strength meant a double measure of responsibility and hardship.

So Elisha received more than a prophet's mantle when Elijah was received by God. In the same way, Jesus has thrown down his cross. Those who pick it up as an act of faith carry the world's rejection forward, and with it the heir's double portion of the Spirit. Ahead lies the finish line and the waiting crown.

Before the Face of God, Book Four, 340–41

Setting Your Sights on Jesus

On our journey through this life, the author of Hebrews encourages us to look to a world to come. The "heroes of faith" of Hebrews 11 were men and women who believed God and his promises about the future. They, like Moses, looked forward to a kingdom that was not yet fully in view, and they persevered because they saw him who is invisible (Heb. 11:27). . . .

If these [heroes of the faith] persevered in faith, how much more should we? They had only tokens of the kingdom; we have seen the kingdom come in Jesus Christ. It should be much easier for us to believe.

Moreover, the "great cloud of witnesses" shows that God has been and will continue to be faithful. The Bible records that these people experienced trials and doubts, but God never let them down. He always kept the preliminary promises he made to them, and he moved the kingdom forward toward fulfillment of his greatest promise. Now that promise has been fulfilled, for the Messiah has come. With this history in mind, we can be absolutely certain that God's future promise of heaven and a new earth will come to pass.

Throughout Hebrews, the author has pointed us to Jesus, the author and perfecter of our faith, who has gone before us and now reaches back to draw us toward perfection. In Hebrews 12:2 he says it again: "Let us fix our eyes on Jesus." Jesus went through cross and trial; so will you. He was crowned with glory and honor; by his grace you will be.

Before the Face of God, Book Four, 346–47

Should I set goals for my life?

The principle of setting goals, setting a mark to strive for, is a healthy thing and has plenty of biblical precedence. People who go wandering aimlessly without any defined goals tend to spin their wheels and get blown to and fro with every wind of doctrine. The very principle of goal setting, I think, is a godly one. But we have to qualify it. Of course, James tells us that we ought not to say with too much confidence that next year I'm going to do such and such, but we should always say, . . . "God willing" (James 4:15). . . .

We spend so much time trying to probe the secret counsel of God when, for all practical purposes, it is none of our business. While there are times when we need to know whether or not a certain thing is in God's approval, we can overdo this quest for God's counsel. . . .

What is pleasing to God is not that much of a mystery: He has given us page after page of instructions as to what pleases him. And so the ultimate goal of our lives is to be faithful in serving him. There is much latitude in the many specific goals we can attain—in career, in family, in hobbies—while following the goals for a godly life as set forth in Scripture.

Now, That's a Good Question! 257–58

Don't Give Up

Sir Winston Churchill returned to Eton, the scene of his childhood education. The students were assembled to hear a speech from Eton's most illustrious alumnus. Churchill was a word merchant, a master of the English language without peer, the king of repartee. . . .

By the time Churchill returned to Eton, his fame as a speaker was already well-known to every British schoolboy. The moment was at hand to hear the great man display his oratory. The assembly was hushed as Churchill approached the podium. He grasped the lectern and thrust out his chin in bulldog ferocity and said, "Never, never, never . . . give up." Then he sat down.

With one sentence he electrified his audience. One wonders how many times in how many young men's secret thoughts those words came back in a moment of crisis, a moment when the fearful totter between fight or flight.

Never give up. This is a message echoed again and again in Holy Writ. . . .

Paul stated it this way: "Forgetting those things which are behind and reaching forward to those things which are ahead, I press toward the goal for the prize of the upward call of God in Christ Jesus" (Phil. 3:13–14 NKJV).

We are called to *press* toward the mark of our high calling. To press is to use exertion. It is to apply pressure. The apostle is calling us to *effort*. The pursuit of righteousness is not a cavalier matter. There is no room for the easy-chair method of sanctification. Determination is important. Effort is important.

Pleasing God, 225–27